A souvenir guide

Stoneywell Cottage
Leicestershire

2

4

8   The Arts and Crafts Movement
10   The architect of Stoneywell
13   The building of Stoneywell

Inside the Cottage
16

17   The Dining Room
18   The Sitting Room
20   The Main Bedroom
22   The Walkthrough Bedroom or Nursery
23   Landing, Bathroom and Loo
24   The Spare Room
25   The Well Room
26   Olympus

A Country Setting
28

30   A Midlands wilderness

Arts and Crafts Continued
32

❀ National Trust

Foreword

Lars Tharp, antiques expert, author, broadcaster and one-time small boy enraptured by the potential for outdoor play in this corner of north-west Leicestershire, shares his personal impressions of Stoneywell.

Some of my earliest memories on coming to England as a six-year-old in 1960 are of weekend trips to the Charnwood Forest. Coming from Copenhagen, to me this vast area of rolling hills, craggy outcrops, ancient woods and mysterious ruins seemed a world crammed with adventures, where the ghosts of dinosaurs, of Robin Hood and others new to me lurked behind every tree, upon every crag and in the shadows of fern and bracken.

It was surely a similar desire for escapism that prompted the two Gimson brothers, Sydney and Mentor, and later their sister Margaret to ask their architect brother Ernest to draw up plans for three summer cottages, 10 miles from the industrial city in which the family iron foundry had forged its name.

Save for its slate roof (replacing the original thatch destroyed in a fire in 1939) with its wizard's hat of a chimney, Stoneywell retains much of its original magic and atmosphere of family holidays and laughing children.

A playful space

I first visited Stoneywell Cottage in 2012. Donald Gimson, grandson of its first residents, Sydney and Jeannie, greeted me warmly at the door and I entered his family's enchanted home. As Donald showed me around the eccentric interior, with its playful obtuse angles, its off-set levels and concealed stairwells, I was overtaken by other memories of my early years in England: the inner and outer landscapes of Winnie the Pooh; the Hundred Acre Wood and the bumpety stairs to bed. Here too was the world of Ratty, Badger and Toad from *Wind in the Willows*, or maybe the perpetual childhood of Peter Pan, or the frisson of Narnia. Here was a magic bedroom, one from which you might escape a pirate attack by leaping safely out of the window, the slope of the hillside rising to meet the first floor a mere 12 inches below. And as all my childhood's imagined worlds swam before me, I spied a rack of books in a bedroom: the Collected Works of Beatrix Potter.

'This is a child's paradise,' I said to Donald. He smiled and began his own reminiscences: of his wife Anne and their children; of visits from their many Gimson kin; of building a

dry-stone fortress on an outcrop; of a soapbox careering down the hillside, its two young occupants screaming in fear and delight as they swerved at the last minute to avoid a rapid tumble into the wood below. Pure *Swallows and Amazons*!

Escapism encapsulated

It's hardly surprising that Stoneywell so vividly recalls such childhood classics, classics written when the citizens of England were escaping from the grime and drudgery of industry, of mass-production and from the trauma of wars. These worlds conjured a childhood idyll in which hair-raising adventures might still be played in safety.

And this is surely as Ernest Gimson intended. The leading light of the second generation of the Arts and Crafts Movement, Gimson's vernacular architecture – filled with the homely tables, chairs and cabinets, the iron, brass and metalwork of the Cotswold School – created something that embodies that rural escape which William Morris longed for and which speaks to us even today: This is How to Live.

Opposite Lars Tharp revisiting childhood memories of the Charnwood Forest

Left Humphrey Gimson straddles the roof of Stoneywell, the cottage a playhouse of childhood delights

Below Stoneywell seen from a child's perspective

An Arts and Crafts Creation

Stoneywell appears the epitome of a rustic cottage, all rough-hewn and deeply bedded into its surroundings, enfolded by ferns and grassy slopes. But although Stoneywell appears organically grown, nothing here was created by chance.

Although really not that old, and maybe a little large to deserve truly the title 'cottage', Stoneywell's inspiration is absolutely within the ancient landscape and vernacular buildings of the Charnwood Forest. It is so much part of the landscape that one ex-local, who'd left before it had been built, said on returning to the area that it was odd that he should have forgotten the old cottage.

Stoneywell was not, however, actually built for someone working in the area, or indeed even as a permanent residence as it later became, but as a summer house for a Leicester industrialist, Sydney Gimson, director of Gimson & Co. Vulcan Works. The engineering company's work included the massive beam engines in the city's Abbey Pumping Station.

In spring Sydney, his wife, Jeannie, and their two sons, Basil and Humphrey, would move from the family's townhouse in Glebe Street, Leicester, to Stoneywell for the summer months. But although they would vacate by late October, they would often return to Stoneywell for Christmas.

Stoneywell is a house of the Arts and Crafts, and arguably the apogee of that movement's style and ideals of function and decoration, so closely does it adhere to their philosophies of site-specific design and use of local materials.

Above A bronze relief of Sydney Ansell Gimson, 1927

Left A Gimson family Christmas at Stoneywell in c.1912

Opposite Stoneywell emerges from the landscape, assembled from its local materials

An appropriate setting

Below The Charnwood Forest's unusually unspoilt nature so close to the city of Leicester led Sydney to this spot

'The proper place for the Arts and Crafts is in the country.' So wrote Charles Robert Ashbee, founder of the Chipping Camden based Arts and Crafts organisation, the Guild of Handicraft.

If Stoneywell's title of cottage is misleading, then forest is even more so, as the Charnwood Forest's 60 square miles are really an area of rocky outcrops, scattered with trees and woods. Many of these rocks are of the very oldest pre-Cambrian type, the same type found in North Wales, and they give the forest a particular character that is unlike the rest of the Midlands. In addition to its picturesque setting, being within 10 miles of the centre of Leicester made the Charnwood Forest popular with Victorian and Edwardian urbanites for recreational camping, walking and cycling trips.

Early such visitors to the forest included Sydney Gimson and his friends, who in the

1870s would spend weekends camping in a loft over a stable. So wild and remote did it seem that the group of friends extinguished their candles early as they worried about being spotted by imagined brigands!

The realisation of a dream

It was another 20 years from these first trips that Sydney bought a plot of land in the forest, together with one for his older brother, Mentor, and a third for another Leicester businessman, James Billson, who was living nearby in the forest at Chitterman Hills Farm. Sydney chose the middle of the three plots because it contained a distinctive outcrop of local granite where he had enjoyed picnics.

Before Sydney had even paid his £140 for the three and a half acres, he and his wife, Jeannie, had instructed his younger brother, the architect and designer Ernest Gimson, to draw up plans for a cottage on the site. Thereafter, it seems, Ernest had a surprisingly free hand in the design of the commission.

Left The Charnwood Forest is a landscape quite unlike the rest of the Midlands

Above Stoneywell's kitchen garden is an enticing view of the good life

The Arts and Crafts Movement

The Arts and Crafts Movement was a reaction to the ills of Victorian industrialisation, and mainly originated with the art critic and romantic, John Ruskin, and that dynamic socialist utopian and businessman, William Morris.

It was a movement of entirely British origins, but was to have substantial international influence, especially in Germany and the United States; and although as an architectural style it was out of fashion by the time of the Second World War, its influence is clearly seen on many designers of more modern times. Terence Conran's statement, for instance, that design ought to be simple, plain and useful, so closely follows Morris's famous and oft-quoted statement of a century earlier: 'Have nothing in your houses that you do not know to be useful, or believe to be beautiful.'

A broad church

But the Arts and Crafts Movement was not only about form and function but also about the maker. To quote Ashbee again: 'Take away the producer's joy; destroy his interest, his care, his thought, turn him into a hack or a machine – in other words destroy his individuality, and the work produced will not be so good.'

Their products were in many disciplines, including jewellery and bookbinding. The furniture could be very simple and of oak, in imitation of country pieces of the 17th century, or exotically inlaid more in the manner of the Spanish or Japanese.

The architecture was similarly eclectic. Some practitioners advocated a strong historicism of the Jacobean or vernacular styles, Stoneywell drawing heavily on the latter. Other architects, such as C. F. A. Voysey and E. S. Prior, were more innovative – Prior in particular, with his use of concrete and also butterfly plan forms.

Above left John Ruskin

Above right William Morris

Left The weaving shed in Morris & Co.'s factory at Merton Abbey, c.1890

A simpler life

However, Arts and Crafts wasn't just a style – it was also a way of life. The idealism of a rediscovery of manual craft went hand in hand with a desire for a return to a simpler life. These reactionary tendencies unsurprisingly left the movement's followers easy game for satire. Osbert Lancaster in his Cultured Cottage cartoon depicts a well-dressed couple at a primitive-looking refectory table. But Arts and Crafts followers, while favouring simplicity, were not puritans and certainly enjoyed revelry, even if it can seem quaint now. For instance, F. L. Griggs, the artist of the drawing of Stoneywell on page 14, was known to sit down at the harpsichord and burst into folksong.

Dancing, singing and drinking ale were popular pastimes. There were often amateur theatricals, too. In fact, Stoneywell's foreman, Detmar Blow, wrote a children's play, recruiting its cast by stopping children in the street outside his London flat – a casting technique that would prove quite impossible today.

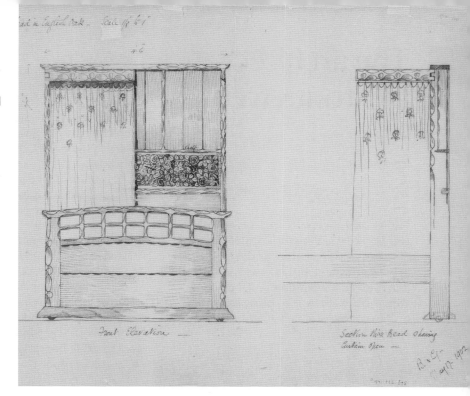

The limitations of simplicity

Ultimately, it was a mixture of harsh financial reality and pragmatism that paved the way for the movement's decline. Ernest Gimson and Ernest and Sidney Barnsley were independently wealthy, so could afford to work slowly and by hand. Most people in Britain were not, and however much they admired such beautiful furniture and houses, they could not afford them.

As for the return to the simple life and the merits of pre-Industrial Age comforts, Ashbee recorded in his 1900 diary: 'The simplification of life is sorely tested by the absence of a bathroom.' The artist, Roger Fry, was even more candid: he'd tried the simple life, but finding it too complicated, had had to give it up!

Nonetheless, Stoneywell's deceptively spare design, its use of immediately local materials, and the intense love felt for it by its owners can teach us a lot.

Above Ernest Barnsley and Ernest Gimson's design for a bedstead in English oak, 1902

Left William Morris design for Trellis wallpaper, 1862

The architect of Stoneywell

Ernest Gimson (1864–1919) was lauded by the architectural historian, Sir Nikolaus Pevsner, as the greatest of the English artist-craftsmen. But he was also described as a thinker, an explorer and a teacher, whose chief aim was to bring back some pride and joy into the work of the British working man.

Aged 19, Ernest had met the influential William Morris when Morris had addressed the Leicester Secular Society – an event for which he stayed at the Gimsons' townhouse. The men stayed up late talking, and Morris was impressed by the young Ernest, upon whom Morris's thinking would have a lifelong influence.

Ernest was at the time articled to the Leicester architect, Isaac Barradale, but later Morris advised him to complete his training in London, and in due course he went to the offices of John Dando Sedding, just along Oxford Street from Morris's shop.

While at Sedding's, he met his future collaborators in the Arts and Crafts, two brothers from Birmingham called Ernest and Sidney Barnsley, and all three became active in Morris's Society for the Protection of Ancient Buildings, along with, among others, a mercurial young man called Detmar Blow (more of whom later).

Escape to the country

Becoming disillusioned with city life, and despairing of ever successfully combining their growing interest in crafts such as chair-making with more conventional architectural practice, the two Ernests and Sidney removed to the Cotswolds in 1893 to live closer to nature. A decade later all three were established near Cirencester, in the

'He was a kindly wizard who could tell us about the plants and animals, stars and cathedrals, politics and history, art and books. Little snorts of appreciation and fun were characteristic of him. As he told, we sat listening and talking by candle and log fire light.'

The Sapperton village schoolmistress about Ernest Gimson

village of Sapperton, in what was described by *Country Life* magazine's long-time editor, H. Avray Tipping, as 'the headquarters of a village industry directed by men with a love and understanding of ancient forms and ancient processes'.

They chose the Cotswolds because of the area's seeming remoteness from everything industrial and pertaining to modern manufacturing and mass production – also, no doubt, because of the strong and attractive vernacular tradition of the local architecture.

A future protégé of Ernest Gimson, Norman Jewson, seeking him out 15 years later, described it even then as a part of the country little known, except to a few architects and artists, and that he had had to hire a donkey outside Cirencester station to carry his bags as he trudged alongside it for the few miles out to Sapperton. But although Gimson made the village his beloved home for quarter of a century, he did not entirely isolate himself professionally in Sapperton, or indeed the Cotswolds.

Opposite Ernest Gimson

Left Ernest Gimson's house at Sapperton, designed by him and built in 1903, photographed by *Country Life*

Below The Gimson and Barnsley families at Pinbury Park, Sapperton, c.1896; from left to right, Sidney Barnsley, Lucy Morley, Ernest Gimson (seated), Alice and her husband Ernest Barnsley, and their two daughters, Mary (who married Norman Jewson) and Ethel

His multiple craft skills, rather than generally his architectural genius, ensured an eclectic range of commissions beyond. These include decorative plasterwork, for example, at Halsey Ricardo's Debenham House in Holland Park, built for the department store's owner – the interiors of which are so often used as television and film sets.

Also, the ivory inlaid ebony stalls for St Andrew's Chapel in Westminster Cathedral; and the distinctive church furniture at St Andrew's, Roker in Sunderland – often described as the Cathedral of the Arts and Crafts. And further afield, although the work did not necessitate visits, furniture for Khartoum Cathedral; and in 1911, a scheme entered in the competition for the new Australian capital, Canberra – alas unsuccessfully.

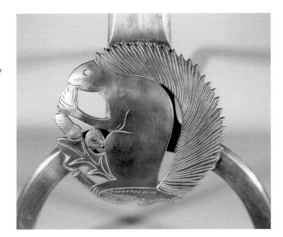

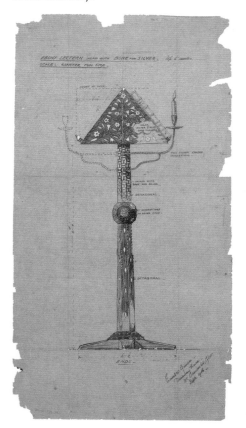

In the way that his friend and fellow architect, Alfred Powell, produced the watercolours for Ernest's idea for Canberra, the intense collaboration for these other projects is a roll call of the greats of the Arts and Crafts: William de Morgan's tiles at Debenham House, Eric Gill's Stations of the Cross at Westminster, the Morris-woven tapestry to Burne-Jones's design at Roker.

Ernest Gimson died at Sapperton aged 54. F. L. Griggs wrote that his untimely death robbed us of an example and an influence which were altogether good, but that Gimson would disapprove of writing about work: he would say that work could be left to itself to secure all the notice and influence it deserved.

'Something made in the country, please.'

Ernest Gimson to a waitress in a Manchester tearoom

Clockwise from bottom left Ernest Gimson worked with many materials, including: this design for an ebony lectern inlaid with bone and silver for St Andrew's Church, Roker; a detail from a polished steel firedog designed by Ernest; and an embroidery of coloured wool on linen

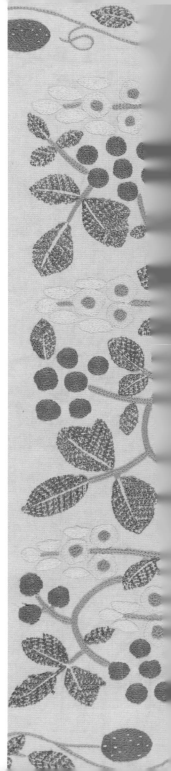

The building of Stoneywell

In spite of Ernest Gimson's move to the Cotswolds, an important Arts and Crafts contemporary and friend called W. R. Lethaby stated that Gimson used to love Leicester and really he was a Leicester man, so he must have been very pleased to be able to return in 1898 to work on Stoneywell Cottage for his brother, Sydney.

In tandem, Ernest worked on the now enlarged Lea Cottage (at the beginning of the drive) for their brother, Mentor, and 10 years later, Rockyfield Cottage for their sister, Margaret. Both cottages have now been sold out of the Gimson family.

Having surveyed the site for Stoneywell, Ernest vociferously opposed Sydney's choices of position for the cottage, insisting instead that it must straddle the plot's far edge, thus going several yards into Mr Billson's neighbouring land. Ernest had his way and Sydney bought the extra strip of land needed.

Emerging from the ground

The rationale behind Ernest Gimson's positioning of the cottage was that it should be a product of its site and emerge from the earth in a truly organic way. With its zig-zag plan and six different floor levels, it's deliberately far removed from being a house simply placed on its plot and constructed by the hand of man.

Stoneywell and Lea Cottages were built by direct labour rather than contract, and Ernest chose his friend and fellow architect, Detmar Blow, as the head mason for both. Blow's taking this more manual role was in accordance with the Arts and Crafts idea that, to quote John Ruskin, 'the painter should grind his own colour; the architect work in the mason's yard with his men'. Hence the divide of white- and blue-collar jobs became blurred, and the craftsman's role exalted.

A photograph from 1898 showing the construction of Stoneywell

Most of the cottage's stones were gathered from what is now its garden. However, in his *Random Memories of the Building of Stoneywell Cottage*, Sydney relates that Blow would sometimes have suitable stones liberated from drystone walls by 'accidentally' reversing a cart into them. He would then have the wall rebuilt minus the desired stone!

The enormous slate lintels over the front door and the fireplaces each weigh about 1½ tons, and were brought on a borrowed pair of wheels from the refuse heaps at the abandoned Swithland Quarry. The roof is also of local Swithland slate. Originally it was straw thatch, but this was destroyed by a fire in 1939 and replaced with local slate. The architect for the repairs was Sydney's son, Humphrey, who had been articled to Edwin Lutyens.

Taking up residence

At Whitsuntide 1899 Sydney took Jeannie and their two children, Basil and Humphrey, to stay for the first time, beginning the pattern of summers and Christmases spent by the Gimsons at Stoneywell before Basil moved there full-time after his retirement from teaching in 1947.

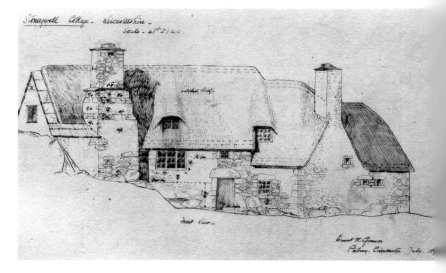

However Basil and his wife, Muriel, were not Stoneywell's first full-time residents. Between his father Sydney's death in 1938 and his own retirement nine years later, Stoneywell was let. For much of the Second World War its tenants were the Lodge family. Doctors Rupert and Kathleen Lodge rented Stoneywell and lived here with their three children after their house in Leicester was hit during a bombing raid in November 1940.

Above Ernest Gimson's drawing of Stoneywell's front elevation, showing the gable built into the rocky bank

Below left The substantial front door lintel of Swithland slate

Below right An engraving of Stoneywell's massive chimney stack by Ernest Gimson's friend, the architectural illustrator F. L. Griggs

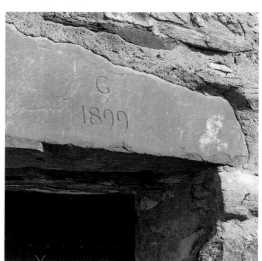

'There is the most extraordinary visual, structural and functional logic to Stoneywell. Of course, there is the other structural and functional logic that says: Build a house of brick on level ground – but that is the difference between building and architecture.'

Nicholas Cooper, architectural historian

The house warming

Early in 1899, and with the initial estimate of £500 now doubled, the cottage was sufficiently complete for Sydney to hold a party for his workmen in the sitting room. A large barrel of beer was sat on the window seat, and Sydney describes in *Random Memories* Detmar Blow's violin playing, and the erratic footprints left in the snow by guests departing in the early hours.

Above The cottage in 1908, some years after completion, successfully bedded into the rock and still with the thatch later destroyed by fire

Inside the Cottage

Stoneywell is a harmonious combination of natural materials.
Note its irregular layout and many changes of level as you explore,
as well as the quality and attention to detail of its craftsmanship.

The Dining Room

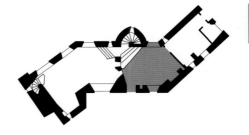

From the front door you go straight into the Dining Room, which was in fact the kitchen until 1953, and had a large bow settle immediately to the right of the door to shelter the occupants from the draught, on the back of which were hooks to hang hats and coats. There was a range for cooking, on which all water was boiled, whether for shaving or making the tea that was specially blended by a Leicester grocer. There was a kitchen table, too, at which Mrs Woolley, the cook, and her daughter, Elsie, the housemaid would work in the 1920s and '30s.

Stoneywell's last owners, Donald Gimson and his wife Anne, decided to create a more modern kitchen behind the door next to the dresser, in what had been the larder, earth closet, coal store and scullery.

Hand-picked pieces

Stoneywell's first owners, Sydney and Jeannie Gimson, decided they didn't want to furnish their new cottage with pieces from their townhouse in Leicester. Sydney wrote: 'We revelled in looking round and choosing suitable things for our new home', and they seem to have done this strictly in accordance with William Morris's previously quoted that you should have nothing in your house that you do not know to be useful, or believe to be beautiful.

Their choices were practical, and as Stoneywell could be cold and damp, especially during the unoccupied winter months, solid furniture was chosen rather than the more sophisticated veneered and inlaid pieces that

they would have had in their townhouse. They bought the rush-seated chairs around the table from Ernest, having watched him turn the chairs' ash legs on a pole lathe. The big oak table, which has a top of a single plank, was made by Ernest's Arts and Crafts collaborator in Gloucestershire, Sidney Barnsley, while the settle mentioned above was by Sidney's elder brother, Ernest Barnsley.

Ernest also built a large Scandinavian-style cupboard for the sitting room, and this can be seen in the Arts and Crafts display at The Wilson, Cheltenham Art Gallery & Museum. The bow settle, however, is now owned by Leicester Museum & Art Gallery, which has an Arts and Crafts gallery at New Walk, and has kindly loaned several pieces to Stoneywell.

Above The Dining Room when it was in use as a kitchen. The draught-excluding settle designed by Ernest can be seen on the right

Opposite
The Dining Room today

The Sitting Room

The broad slate steps lead up to the Sitting Room. Note the stoneware hot-water bottles placed as seen in an early photograph and confirming the comment in *Small Country Houses of To-day* (1922) that 'one suspects [it] is in cold weather very cold'. There was no central heating until 1969, its installation only being made possible by the cottage's connection to mains water two years earlier. This crank-shaped room divides naturally into two, although this would previously have been more pronounced when the dining table ran across its width. The room's near end, with its window seat and garden view, forms a daytime sitting room, whereas that beyond is focused around the fire for evening relaxation.

Above The inglenook fire provided warmth in the cooler months; central heating was not installed until 1969

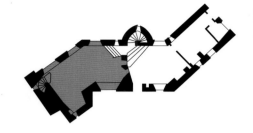

Purpose-made pieces

The two rush-seated chairs were made for the National Trust by Lawrence Neal, who is descended by a series of apprenticeships from Ernest Gimson, and still uses many of Gimson's tools. These chairs are to the same design as those made for Bedales School's library – another very fine building by Ernest Gimson.

Behind the wireless is a small games cupboard in the wall. Inside you will find the table-tennis net used on the dining table. Although the table is the same length as a standard table-tennis table, it is rather narrower, thus making for a challenging game.

Donald Gimson kept more toys in the under-seat drawer of the Orkney chair on the rear wall. These curious chairs were originally made from driftwood and seagrass woven into ropes. They were very fashionable craft items at the beginning of the 20th century, and were stocked by smart department stores.

Around the fireside

Perhaps because of the cottage's position against the bank, the inglenook fire smoked badly. To overcome this problem the fire-block stiles you see today were fitted quite early on. They were recently rediscovered outside being reused as the base of the wood store, and refitted in the fireplace.

During the original construction of the fireplace, a mason had been about to chisel off the protruding slate on the left when Detmar Blow instructed: 'No, leave it, it'll serve for Sydney's smoke shelf.' A small thing perhaps, but representative of the kind of attention to detail on a human scale found in Arts and Crafts.

The steep and narrow steps opposite lead up to the Main Bedroom, and Donald Gimson remembers his grandfather ascending them nightly into his late seventies.

Right The protruding slate saved for Sydney Gimson's tobacco jar

The Main Bedroom

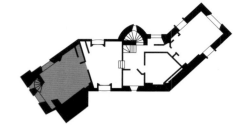

Owing to Stoneywell's many levels, it's possible to step straight into the garden from the window on the gable end – something that was taken advantage of by many children, especially when playing tag.

Look closely at the walnut coffer raised up by the window, particularly its carved bands. Its designer, Joseph Armitage, was especially brilliant at carving plants and flowers in relief. In fact, in 1935 he entered the National Trust's competition to design the Trust's logo, and won with just a slight variation on the oak leaves and acorns you see here on the coffer's right-hand end.

The wonderful walnut secretaire-chest is more of a townhouse piece. It was made for Basil Gimson's 21st birthday by Sidney Barnsley, and was originally in the family's Leicester house, only being brought to Stoneywell from Bedales following Basil Gimson's retirement in 1947.

Linoleum was laid over Stoneywell's regionally characteristic lime ash floors from about 1940 to 1970. Fortunately, the manufacturers, who remain in business, still produce a similar cork-based product in a comparable colour to the original, so it has been possible to lay it again.

Left The coffer designed by Joseph Armitage features a motif familiar to National Trust supporters

Right The Main Bedroom window on the first floor through which it is possible to step out onto the bank

The Walkthrough Bedroom or Nursery

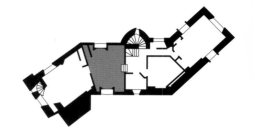

In Sydney Gimson's time this is where Mrs Woolley and Elsie slept, the double bed in the Main Bedroom at that time having its head towards the interconnecting door. In the 1950s it became a nursery for Donald and Anne's daughter, Sally.

The wardrobe in this room, as indeed in the other bedrooms, was fitted when the cottage was rebuilt after the fire of 1939. Previously, it seems family and guests could only have brought essential clothing with them, as there was little storage space.

The colourful print over the door to the landing is from a painting by a Viennese schoolchild, and was sold to raise money by the Red Cross following the First World War. There are two smaller but similar works on the opposite wall. During the First World War Sydney was very involved in helping Belgian refugees who'd fled the German advance in 1914. Assistance was given to more than a thousand in Leicester alone, with a hundred houses being given over to the refugees. Because they were of several different faiths, it was decided least controversial to appoint Sydney – a professed atheist – to undertake this pastoral work. He seems to have been so successful in this role that a Belgian Catholic priest joked to him: 'You will never be able to speak against the confessional again, for you are now the Father Confessor to all these Belgians.' Sydney's work was recognised by the award of the Albert Medal from H. M. the King of the Belgians, Albert I.

Left The view through the Walkthrough Bedroom

Right This high chair was made to a design by Ernest Gimson

Landing, Bathroom and Loo

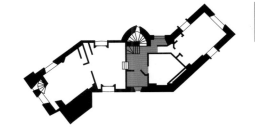

In 1938 Stoneywell was wired for electricity, and this meant rainwater could be pumped to roof tanks and heated for baths. Consequently, the landing was partitioned to create this bathroom which, on account of its black and white panels, Donald believed seemed very Jazz Age compared to the rest of the cottage.

The joiner, Mr W. Jones from Barrow-on-Soar, had only just finished panelling the bathroom when an electrical fault in the roof set fire to the thatch. Although nearly all the cottage's contents were saved, the roof and parts of the first floor, including the Bathroom, were badly damaged. For many months, six days a week, Mr Jones made the 25-mile round trip on his bicycle to undertake repairs. Out of economy, Ernest Gimson had originally had all the doors made of chestnut, which looks very similar to oak. Mr Jones, however, purchased oak coffin boards from an undertaker to replace the burnt door into the Walkthrough Bedroom.

Below The modern convenience of the Bathroom must have seemed markedly different from the rigorous simplicity elsewhere in the cottage

The Spare Room

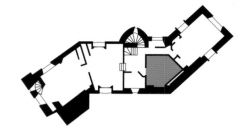

If you haven't already noticed them elsewhere in the cottage, do look closely at the wonderful, traditional door latch in this room – a great quality of Stoneywell's detail, in common with its furniture, is that it's so pleasing to the touch as well as being beautiful to look at.

On the left-hand wall of this curiously five-sided room is a photograph of J. H. Badley. Known as The Chief, Badley founded and was for many years headmaster of the progressive Bedales School in Hampshire. Basil and Donald were both educated there; Basil subsequently also worked there as senior maths master and latterly as second master. The school had strong Arts and Crafts values, believing in the

Left The simple but carefully crafted latch of the Spare Room

Below left A watercolour of Bedales library, designed by Ernest Gimson, painted by the school's one-time art master

education of 'head, heart and hand'. These ideals are embodied in both the appearance and construction of many of the school's buildings, especially of course Ernest Gimson's library and the assembly hall, built by Geoffrey Lupton, a past pupil at Bedales.

The watercolour on the far wall is by Bedales' art master, Innes Meo, and in fact shows Ernest Gimson's wonderful library. Meo taught Donald Gimson in the 1930s. The picture was bought from the art master by Donald's father, Basil, when he too was a master at the school.

The oak double bed was made by Sidney Barnsley, and is one of Stoneywell's original pieces.

The Well Room

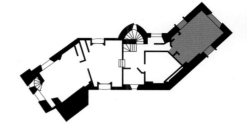

So called because one steps down into it, rather than for any known health reason, this bedroom was used from the 1950s by Donald's son, Roger. However, in the cottage's earlier days as a summerhouse, it was more often a visiting family's dormitory.

Not unusually perhaps for a schoolmaster, Basil Gimson was a great buyer of second-hand books, and so regularly ran out of shelf space. To meet demand, he commissioned Edward Barnsley to make the bookcases that fit into the eaves. Edward was Sidney Barnsley's son, and his workshops at Froxfield in Hampshire continue to produce very high-quality furniture for the international market.

The two cane chairs are by the Leicester firm of Dryad, which was set up in 1907. If you're visiting in summer, you'll also see a pair of reclining Dryad chairs and a table in the garden. The firm's founder, Harry Peach, was a friend of Sydney Gimson, and the two men shared many ideals concerning design and education. Peach was essentially reviving the traditional Leicestershire craft of basket making, but following Continental fashions. During the Great War they turned production to shell, gun and balloon baskets, and even early aircraft seats. Sadly, the American invention of Lloyd Loom woven paper put an end to Dryad's cane furniture production, although the firm was subsequently successful as Dryad Handicrafts.

Above The bookcases were made to fit snugly into the eaves

Left The Well Room in the early 1900s

Olympus

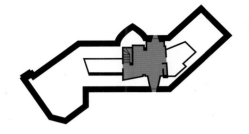

The top-floor bedroom, so called because Mount Olympus is the highest point in the ancient Greek world, was used by many of Stoneywell's visitors, but for 12 years from the mid-1920s this was Donald's Aunt Nora's room. Half-sister of his mother, Muriel, she helped look after Stoneywell after the death of his grandmother, Jeannie. Before the rebuild after the fire of 1939, the room was smaller and access was by ladder from the Nursery.

Note the Arthur Ransome novels on the shelf to the left of the wardrobe. These replace the ones kept by Donald Gimson when he left, each of which he'd been sent by his uncle on publication. The books' subjects must be especially redolent of childhood summer holidays at Stoneywell.

Married well?
Looking out towards the lane, you will see the conically roofed Well House, which is shared with Lea Cottage. In front is the chilly spring-fed plunge pool in which earlier Gimson brides were made to jump to show their mettle!

Opposite Olympus has the furthest views of the gardens and surrounding countryside

Left From Olympus and the Landing it is a steep and winding descent to the Dining Room

A Country Setting

Just as Stoneywell Cottage is designed to appear as if organically grown among the rocky outcrops of the Charnwood Forest, the garden and outlying areas blend seamlessly with this wild-looking landscape.

An 1899 watercolour (see front cover) shows the cottage in its immediate setting. The ground is rough and gorse covered, the path worn and strewn with granite pebbles. This is both the physical and philosophical setting of the cottage, these the organic building blocks from which it was constructed.

Shortly after the Stables were built, Sydney had two varieties of daffodil planted in the area between the road and the rocky outcrop. Over more than 100 years, these have been allowed to seed and multiply in the rough grass. In the spring they form a vast yellow carpet of many thousands of flowers.

Sydney was a keen tennis player and between 1903 and 1905 he had a grass tennis court made by blasting the rock, levelling (several times), seeding and then fencing in. Later, two vegetable gardens were dug and surrounded by stone walls to keep the rabbits out.

Donald Gimson remembers his grandfather Sydney employing a gardener, George Richardson, from nearby Newtown Linford. He worked three days a week, all year round, and Sydney would visit weekly during winter to pay him and return to Leicester with any produce.

Donald recalls Richardson fondly as being instrumental in developing his love of the country and its ways. He knew where to find the slow worms and how to skin a rabbit, how to fell trees and split them to make posts and rails for fencing, and all the useful things one wanted to know. He continued as gardener for the next two generations of the Gimson family.

Keen gardeners

Donald and Anne Gimson were passionate gardeners and, unlike Sydney, year-round residents. Therefore, over more than 50 years they domesticated the areas closer to the cottage by planting them with species such as heathers, rhododendrons, azaleas, magnolias and those herbaceous plants which are tolerant of acid soil.

During the summer, Anne would start work in the garden shortly after breakfast and continue till dusk. She compiled extensive gardening notes of which the National Trust has copies. She was also an accomplished flower arranger, using almost exclusively what grew in the garden to create Constance Spry-form displays.

Above The view over the drystone wall into the Tennis Court

Left Soft foliage in the Walled Garden

Opposite Drifts of daffodils in front of the Stables

A Midlands wilderness

The 11 acres of woodland abutting the garden can be wandered in and are full of bluebells in the spring. The woods are classified as ancient and form part of the Ulverscroft Valley Site of Special Scientific Interest. They were bought in the 1920s when the Bradgate Estate was auctioned.

Halfway along the garden going back towards the Stables is the Fort, which you will have passed as you approached the cottage. Basil and Humphrey Gimson, when they were teenagers, added drystone walls to the natural outcrop to create a pretend fort to play in. Several generations of young children have thatched it each year with bracken and learned early climbing skills on the rock face.

The Stables were built three years after the cottage, and have been even less altered over time than the cottage has. They only housed horses for a short while as Sydney, being an engineer, was an early convert to motoring. The tearoom is in the old laundry, and the original copper is being relit in winter for warmth.

Above **The Fort has been stormed and defended by generations of children**

Left **The entrance to acres of woodland to be explored**

Right The weathercock
designed by Ernest
and given as a birthday
present to Sydney

Make sure you look up to see the weathercock
over the gable-end steps, also designed by
Ernest Gimson. It was a surprise birthday
present from Jeannie's elder sister, Nellie, to
Sydney early in the 20th century. Jeannie
walked him past it several times, but only when
she stared up at it did he notice it.

Because there are maternity roosts for
pipistrelle and brown long-eared bats, the two
small rooms up the steps on the gable end have
been sealed off. The further one was used by
Humphrey for bookbinding, while the one
nearer the steps was once Sydney's workshop.

Arts and Crafts Continued

When, aged 29, Donald Gimson inherited Stoneywell, and he and Anne moved here full-time, it wasn't merely to become custodians of an Arts and Crafts masterpiece. It might appear to the casual observer that, in comparison to the major work that the couple did in the garden, they did relatively little to the cottage beyond creating a now seemingly old-fashioned kitchen and installing central heating. However, the real explanation for this cautious approach lies deeper and further back in time.

Although Donald never knew his grandfather's younger brother, Ernest, every summer was spent with his grandparents at Stoneywell. The Arts and Crafts mantle was truly taken up early in his school days at the junior school for Bedales, when he was first taught the correct use of woodworking tools.

On one of the Trust's early visits to Stoneywell, Donald pointed out two small

tables to the Trust's curator and author of this guidebook, Simon Chesters Thompson. 'I made this one,' he said, 'when I was seven, and that one when I was 70,' adding, 'I didn't learn much in between, did I?' However, what was surprising during that tour was not so much the precociousness of the earlier-made piece, but something he said later.

When asked about the rather stubby legs on an oak bed made by Ernest, Donald said that he'd sawn them off because his wife hadn't been especially tall. Noting the surprise that statement provoked, he followed up with: 'Well, it wasn't fit for purpose with long legs!' And of course he was right; a nice-looking bed that's uncomfortably high isn't much more use than a gold watch that's only right twice a day – pure Arts and Crafts rationale in the manner of W. R. Lethaby's axiom that a work of art is a well-made boot!

Above Three generations of the Gimsons at Stoneywell: (top to bottom) Basil, Sydney and Donald

Left Stoneywell now welcomes a new generation of visitors

Opposite The Orkney chair in the drawer of which Donald stowed toys